Action for the Environment

Food for All

Rufus Bellamy

FRANKLIN WATTS
LONDON • SYDNEY

This edition 2006

Franklin Watts
338 Euston Road
London NW1 3BH

Franklin Watts Australia
Level 17/207 Kent Street
Sydney, NSW 2000

ISBN: 978 0 7496 6946 1

Dewey Classification: 363.8

A CIP catalogue record for this book is
available from the British Library

Printed in Malaysia

Editor: Adrian Cole
Design: Proof Books
Art Director: Jonathan Hair
Picture Research: Kathy Lockley

Acknowledgements
A.Arbib-Christian Aid/Still Pictures Cover b, 7.
ARS, USDA /Photo by Jack Dykinga 10, /Photo
by Keith Weller 9 t, /Photo by Scott Bauer 18 b,
20, 28, /Photo by Susan Boyer 13 t. Matthew
Bolton/Ecoscene 4 t. Stephen Coyne/Ecoscene 13
b. Daniel Dancer/Still Pictures 2, 12. (c) Digital
Vision Ltd. All rights reserved 21 t. Adrian
Dorst/Still Pictures 18 t. Mark Edwards/ Still
Pictures 8, 29, 31. (c) Fairtrade Foundation 27.
(c) F.A.O. 5r. Friends of the Earth England, Wales
& Northern Ireland 15 b. Ron Giling/ Still
Pictures 26. Jim Holmes 9 b. ITDG/ZUL 23,
/Annie Bungeroth 17, /Janet Boston 15 t, 16.
Christine Osborne/Ecoscene 22. PA Photos 4 b, 5.
Rex Features 25 b. Sea Spring Photos/ Ecoscene
Cover tl. Jorgen Schytte/Still Pictures 25 t.
Friedrich Stark/Still Pictures 1, 6, 24. Charlotte
Thege/Still Pictures 11. (c) 2004 Topham
Picturepoint 14. Western Australia Fishing
Industry/MSC 19. (c) W.H.O./P. Virot 21b. David
Wootton Photography/Ecoscene Cover tr.

Franklin Watts is a division of
Hachette Children's Books.

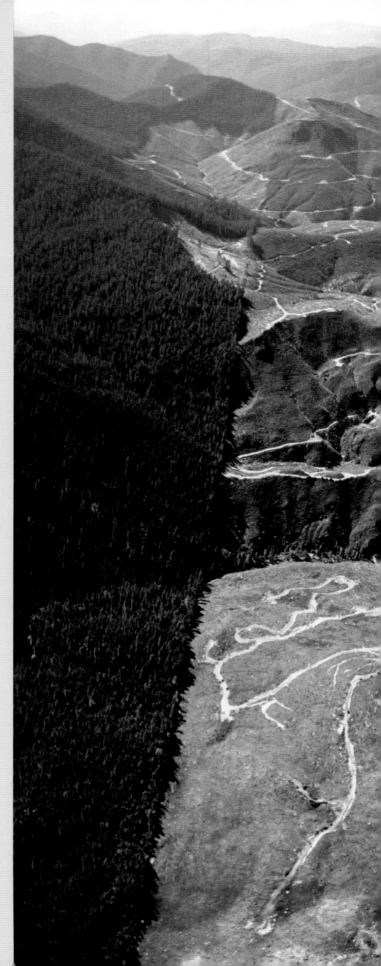

Contents

Feeding the world

It seems incredible that in a world where there are shops full of food some people still go hungry. In fact, more than 800 million people around the world do not have enough to eat.

A busy food market in Guatemala. Food is produced and sold all over the world, but not everyone can access it or afford to buy it.

WORLD HUNGER

People starve if they cannot get, grow or buy enough healthy and nutritious food. This mainly happens in areas of the developing world where many people are very poor. In these countries, there are very few safeguards to help feed people if their crops fail, or if they run out of money to buy food and get into debt.

Food handouts on World Food Day in Pakistan. People in some parts of the world rely on food aid.

FIGHTING THE PROBLEM

To fight hunger many people are tackling key environmental problems, such as soil loss and drought, which cause food crops and animals to die. Many people are also working to tackle poverty and to make sure that food is fairly distributed to the poor and hungry.

WORLD FOOD DAY

Action stations

At the 2002 World Food Summit in Rome, Italy, governments from around the world promised to reduce the total number of hungry people by 50% by the year 2015. To encourage action, World Food Day takes place on 16th October every year. People around the world look at food issues and some take part in marches and protests. Log on to the website (www.fao.org/wfd) and see what you can do to help.

Protesters outside a McDonald's restaurant in Hong Kong on World Food Day. They are concerned that food is not distributed fairly around the world.

Famine relief

Wars, natural disasters and other crises often cause millions of people to starve. Such situations can occur suddenly and cause a famine. Immediate solutions are needed to stop people becoming ill and dying of starvation.

SURVIVING FAMINE

In a famine, aid organisations help feed those people without food by bringing in emergency food and water supplies. Such 'famine relief' is vital. However, it is only a short-term solution.

These children in Ethiopia would rather eat food bought in the local market. However, because of drought and war, there is no food to buy and they are forced to queue for emergency food.

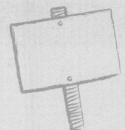

Action stations

Ethiopia is often struck by famine. In 2002 the rains failed or were late, causing a drought. Crops suffered and 11 million Ethiopians faced hunger and starvation. To assist those in danger, Oxfam and other aid groups distributed over 1 million tons of food aid (including wheat, cooking oil and high-protein food) sent by countries around the world.

Famine relief in Africa. Severe drought has destroyed crops and farmland in many parts of Africa. Without emergency food aid many people would starve.

LOOKING FOR ANSWERS

Many organisations, such as Oxfam, are looking for long-term answers to the problems that create hunger and famine. They help people to get land and work, and to secure better trading deals (see pages 26–27). This allows them to grow and buy the food they need.

Growing more food

Farmers around the world try many different ways to produce enough food to feed themselves and the world's rapidly growing population. Some of the methods they use are better for the environment than others.

Intercropping, such as this in Cuba, can help to improve the quality of the soil.

A MIXED HARVEST

In some countries farmers plant a number of different crops in each field at a time. This is called intercropping and it helps farmers produce more types of food. It can also reduce the amount of damage caused by pests and diseases because they will often only affect one particular crop.

EXPENSIVE SOLUTIONS

In the 1970s, scientists developed new 'high-yield' forms of rice and wheat that were designed to feed the world's rapidly growing population. Unfortunately, poor farmers cannot easily afford the machines and chemicals needed for most high-yield crops.

Farm chemicals are not only expensive, but can also harm the environment.

Action stations

In Vietnam, fish farmers have found a very effective way of producing more food from their fishponds. By keeping ducks on their ponds, these farmers can produce up to 40% more fish. This is because the waste the ducks produce helps to feed the fish. Farmers get two types of food (fish and duck meat) from each pond and do not have to spend much money on fish food.

Ducks on this pond in Vietnam help feed the fish and are also a valuable source of food.

Caring for the soil

In regions such as South America and Africa, soil has been lost because of erosion caused by wind, rain and grazing animals. Without soil most crops cannot grow, but now farmers are fighting back to save their land.

This scientist is monitoring the level of soil erosion in a field. Without plants and trees to hold soil together it is easily washed away.

HOLDING SOIL TOGETHER

In areas, such as parts of China, farmers are planting shrubs and trees on their land to hold the soil together. Some farmers in South America have pioneered new ways of planting crops so that they do not need to plough their fields. This stops soil erosion because the land is disturbed as little as possible.

FEEDING SOIL

Soil contains nutrients that plants need. If crops are grown in one area of soil year after year, the nutrients are used up and must be replaced. This can be done with artificial chemicals, called fertilisers, but these are expensive. They can also pollute the environment because they wash into rivers and poison the wildlife. Many farmers use animal waste and other natural ways to fertilise their soil.

These women in Africa are going to plant aloe in a field. The plants will help to stop soil erosion by holding the soil together.

Action stations

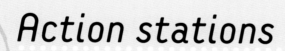

Many farmers, in regions such as sub-Saharan Africa, earn less than £1 a day so they cannot afford to buy man-made chemicals to fertilise their land. Some of them grow special plants called legumes that put vital chemicals back into the soil. Other shrubs, such as aloe, are also planted to form barriers that stop soil erosion.

Trees and food

Forests and woodlands are very important because they help farmers to grow food. They stop soil erosion and increase moisture levels in the soil. Forests themselves are also an incredibly important source of food, fuel and other raw materials for many people.

TREES FOR CROPS

In many countries forests are being destroyed at a very worrying rate. However, campaign groups are working to protect more forests, and farmers and other landowners are planting new trees and hedges. Trees can help crops to grow. For example, trees are grown to provide shelter for crops and so improve harvests in many areas.

A boundary between forest and cleared land. For years farmers have cut down trees to make room for crops and cattle. But now some forests are being replanted.

TREES HELP ANIMALS

Millions of farmers also depend on trees to provide food and shelter for their animals. For example, in West Virginia in the USA, dairy farmers keep trees on their pastures to protect cattle from the hot sun. This has been shown to improve the amount of milk the cows produce.

Planting trees provides shade for cattle. The fruit of some trees can also be sold.

Action stations

In countries such as Indonesia, farmers and scientists are working together to discover the best way to grow crops alongside trees. They have found that this type of farming — called agroforestry — helps to protect the environment. It can also supply people with a greater variety of food and other useful resources including berries, nuts and wood.

This farmer is growing a variety of crops alongside trees, which hold the soil together and shelter the crops from strong winds.

13

Stopping pests and diseases

A swarm of locusts can eat a field of crops in hours, while foot-and-mouth disease can harm millions of farm animals. Pests and diseases such as these are major causes of food loss.

A locust swarm in Ethiopia. These insects will eat the farmer's crop within hours – leaving him without any food to eat or sell.

KILLER BUGS

Scientists have developed many solutions to help stop food loss caused by pests and diseases. For example, chemical sprays that kill pests and weeds, and animal vaccinations that stop disease. Although these help, they cost a lot of money and can cause soil and water pollution.

FRIENDLY FIGHTERS

Today, farmers in countries such as Indonesia are battling pests by releasing 'friendly' animals, such as spiders, to eat them. Farmers in other parts of the world are extracting naturally occurring pesticides from plants. These 'natural' approaches mean that farmers can use fewer chemicals to keep their crops healthy, which reduces the environmental damage they cause.

This farmer is extracting a naturally occurring pesticide from a type of cactus.

Action stations

Scientists have developed a way of artificially producing crops with new properties. Some of these 'genetically modified' (GM) crops have been designed to make it easier for farmers to kill pests and weeds. But many environmental groups, including Friends of the Earth International, are campaigning against GM crops. They believe GM crops will contaminate and harm the natural environment.

A GM food protest in France. Many people think that growing GM food could harm wildlife and be bad for human health.

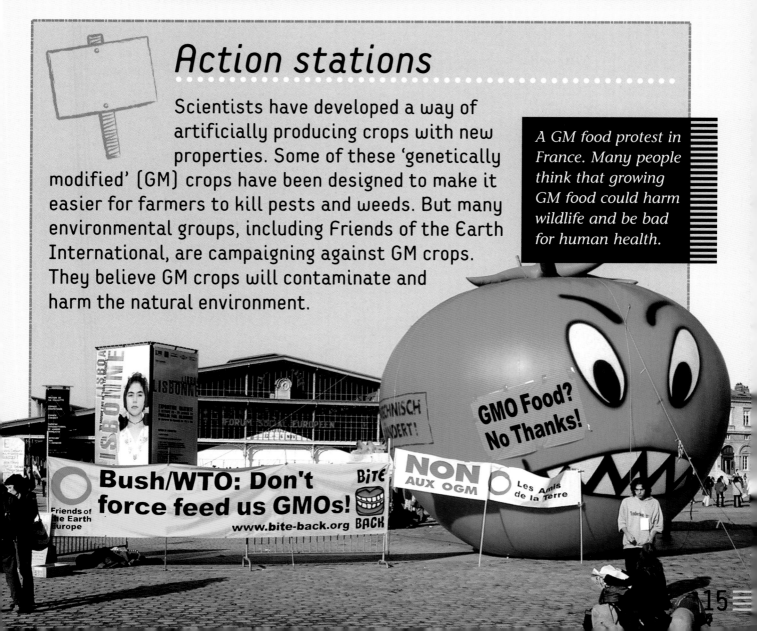

Water for life

Without enough water, crops cannot grow and people and farm animals die. Water shortage is one of the biggest problems facing farmers. This is not only the case in the developing world, but also in the developed world.

LETTING WATER WORK

Farmers in countries with a water shortage save water using different techniques. For example, some create terraces in their fields to stop water running off the land, which gives the water time to sink in. Others put down mulch to stop water evaporating (turning into water vapour) from the surface. Saving water like this helps farmers to grow more food.

Adding mulch to a terraced field in Zimbabwe. These methods stop water run-off and evaporation.

CONSERVING WATER

Many farmers water their crops using large irrigation systems. But these systems use lots of water from rivers and lakes, which can become dry. New ways of watering crops have recently been introduced. These include drip-feed pipes that use up to 80% less water. They release the water slowly so that it does not run off the land or evaporate quickly.

Action stations

In Mexico, where water is scarce, a new irrigation programme has been set up with a loan from the World Bank. The Integrated Irrigation Modernisation Project will provide £170 million to help around 110,000 farmers build irrigation ditches and pipelines. It is vital that the project does not lead to water wastage, so it will also focus on reducing water loss and increasing efficiency.

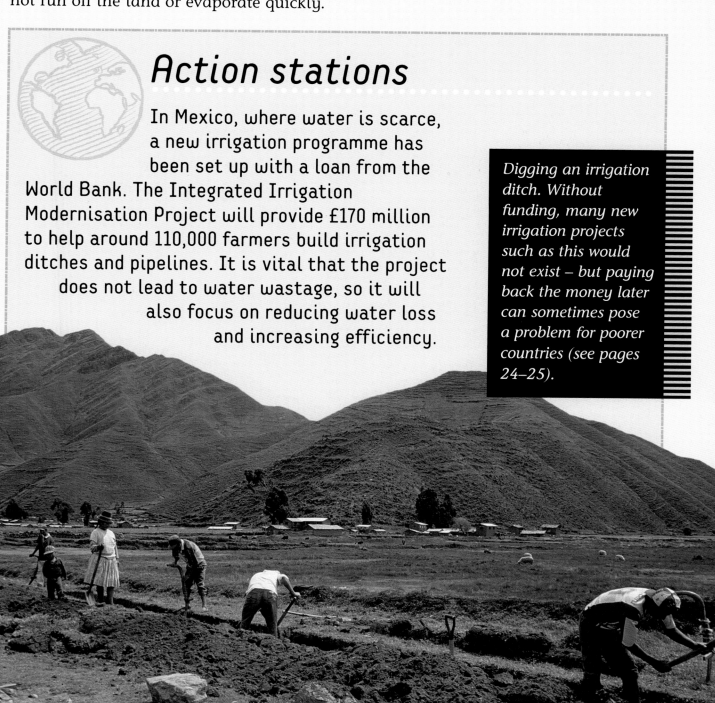

Digging an irrigation ditch. Without funding, many new irrigation projects such as this would not exist – but paying back the money later can sometimes pose a problem for poorer countries (see pages 24–25).

Saving the seas

Many people rely on fish and other seafood as a major source of food. Unfortunately, problems caused by sea pollution and overfishing have meant that the numbers of fish are falling. Fishermen are finding it harder and harder to catch what they need.

Commercial fishing like this is placing a huge strain on the sea's natural resources.

STOPPING THE POLLUTERS

Governments around the world are trying to reduce sea pollution, which threatens fish stocks. For example, France and Italy (two of the biggest polluters of the Mediterranean Sea) have signed agreements with other Mediterranean countries to reduce the amount of sea pollution they create.

Testing for river pollution. A lot of water pollution enters the seas via rivers, so it is important to monitor river water quality.

SAVING FISH STOCKS

More than 70% of the world's fishing areas now have worryingly low levels of fish. At the 2002 World Summit for Sustainable Development held in Johannesburg, South Africa, governments from all over the world agreed to try and reduce the amount of fish their countries' fishing fleets catch.

Action stations

The Marine Stewardship Council (MSC) is funded by charitable events and organisations around the world. It is trying to make fishing less destructive by working with fishing communities and businesses. The MSC has introduced a food packaging label for fish and seafood that shows it has been caught in a way that does not damage fish stocks or habitats.

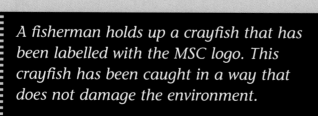

A fisherman holds up a crayfish that has been labelled with the MSC logo. This crayfish has been caught in a way that does not damage the environment.

Safe food

To keep people active and healthy, food must be nutritious and safe. Food can become infected with bacteria or poisoned by pesticides. This happens if food is not handled, stored or transported properly.

FOOD CONTAMINATION

More than 2 million people, mainly in developing countries, die each year from diseases carried by contaminated food and water. In many countries health advisors show people how to prepare and cook food so that it is safe to eat. Other sources of food contamination include pesticides.

PESTICIDE USE

Some pesticides can harm the environment and also damage people's health. In the developed world, testing ensures that food is not contaminated. However, environmental groups believe that more food should be produced organically; without the use of artificial chemicals.

This scientist has collected broccoli to test it for pesticide levels.

FOOD SAFETY

Many countries in the developing world are now trying to introduce tougher food safety checks, and other safeguards such as refrigerating food in transit. Some countries in the European Union have recently introduced cattle passports and tags. These measures should help stop the spread of diseases, such as foot-and-mouth and BSE.

The health of animals, such as these piglets, is closely monitored to stop the spread of disease.

Action stations

The World Health Organisation (WHO) is just one of many groups that provides people all over the world with food safety education. By improving food hygiene, handling and storage, the WHO hopes to reduce the outbreak and spread of food-related diseases.

The WHO organises many events throughout the world. This celebration is part of an education day held in Geneva, Switzerland.

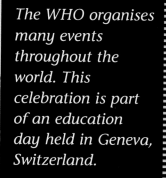

Sustainable solutions

Many organisations help farmers in the developing world get the knowledge, resources and tools they need to grow food, protect the land and improve their quality of life. These are all part of a 'sustainable solution' that helps farmers get the most from their land over many years.

FARMING EDUCATION

Education is very important. For example, in Kenya, a recent national campaign giving farmers advice on environmentally-friendly farming techniques dramatically increased the amount of maize, beans and potatoes the country produced.

This farming project in Africa brings together new farming techniques with the skills of local people. Projects like this can increase the amount of food produced by farms.

This woman from Fadzavanhu Enterprises proudly holds up jars of peanut butter. Instead of selling their crops, small-scale farmers can make more money by creating and selling a product of their own.

Action stations

Farmers can make a much better livelihood from their farms if they turn their crops into new products. For example, peanut farmers in Zimbabwe formed Fadzavanhu Enterprises, which produces peanut butter. To help such projects succeed, many organisations, such as 'Practical Solutions' (formerly the Intermediate Technology Development Group), offer training and resources for small-scale farmers. This type of help not only improves the farmers' profits, but also provides work for other villagers.

Reducing poverty and debt

Poverty is caused by many problems, including high unemployment, corruption, crime, discrimination, and a lack of education and medical help. It often leads to hunger. Many organisations work to help people overcome poverty.

LANDLESSNESS

One important cause of poverty and hunger is landlessness. Some people are forced off their land. For example, large international companies take over small farms and use the land to grow 'cash crops', such as cotton. In South America, the AVINA Foundation has partnered local people to help them get land, while promoting respect for the environment.

A slum in Manila, the Philippines. People who are forced off the land often move to cities to find work. This can lead to more poverty and hunger.

MICRO LOANS

Many groups also help people with small financial loans. Often only a small amount of money is needed to improve a person's livelihood. Oxfam gives 'micro loans' to people in Africa, including farmers. These loans are used to buy tools or machinery, and can be repaid quickly. They help farmers produce enough food to feed their families and make money by selling any surplus.

This tailor bought a sewing machine with a micro loan.

Action stations

Public protests like this one for 'kill the debt' led to the cancellation of £20 billion of debt.

Many poor countries owe wealthy countries massive amounts of money. A lot of cash crops are exported just to pay off this 'third world debt'. The International Jubilee 2000 campaign asked the leaders of rich nations to cancel the crippling debts of the poorest countries. Because of massive public pressure, which has included many protest marches, so far about £20 billion of debts have been cancelled.

Fair trade

One of the main reasons many farmers in the developing world are poor and go hungry is because they do not have much bargaining power. This means that they often do not get a fair price for their crops. Improving trade can reduce poverty.

A FAIR PRICE

Organisations, such as the Fairtrade Foundation and Traidcraft, are now working directly with farmers to help them trade and get a 'fair' price for their crops (see opposite page). This type of fair trade gives poor farmers the chance to improve their livelihood because it increases their income. They can then invest in their land, store extra food and be better prepared for natural disasters, such as droughts.

Fair trade benefits individual growers and labourers, like this woman, who work on farms.

TRADING TO TACKLE POVERTY

Fair trade can help reduce poverty in developing countries. As countries become richer, more people get jobs that do not depend heavily on farming. These jobs give people more money to buy food from wherever it is available. Therefore they do not have to go hungry even if national crops fail. Many campaigners hope that fair trade could be one long-term solution to hunger for many people in developing countries.

Action stations

You can help farmers in the developing world by buying 'fair trade' products such as coffee, tea and chocolate — just look out for the logo (right). The companies trading these products make sure that the farmers who produce the raw materials get a much better or 'fair' price for them. Many also help the farmers they trade with to improve workers' safety and to protect the environment.

FAIRTRADE

The Fairtrade Foundation logo (above) is recognised worldwide. Food that carries the logo has been bought from farmers at a fair price.

Future challenges

In the next 50 years, the world's population is expected to grow by over 2 billion people. This, and other problems, will make it even more difficult to feed everyone and protect the environment.

HEALTH PROBLEMS

AIDS has killed many farmers and labourers in the developing world, leaving a shortage of healthy people to grow food. So far there has been some limited success in getting affordable drugs to the poor, but AIDS is far from beaten.

GLOBAL WARMING

Food production faces another major challenge – global warming. This is thought to be caused by human activities, such as burning fossil fuels. An increase in global temperature could destroy many crops, especially those in countries that already experience droughts and floods.

Scientists are closely monitoring global weather patterns. The effects of global warming could change food production worldwide.

COLLECTING SEEDS

Many farmers only rely on one variety of each crop that they grow. This means that a disease can wipe out a whole crop in one go. Scientists are now working with farmers in regions such as the Middle East to collect the seeds of many different wild varieties of each crop. These can be used to breed new crops that will resist disease.

This class provides these Indian women with practical family planning advice.

Action stations

To help couples plan how many babies they have, many organisations provide family planning advice and support. This gives women the opportunity to get education and employment, and also makes it easier for families to feed their children. These education programmes will help to reduce the rate of world population growth in the future. They are part of the solution to world hunger and starvation.

Glossary

Agroforestry A way of growing food in which farmers plant crops next to trees.

AIDS (Acquired Immune Deficiency Syndrome) A serious illness that causes death. It stops the body protecting itself from other diseases.

Aloe A plant with fleshy spiny-toothed leaves that grows in Africa.

BSE (Bovine Spongiform Encephalopathy) A fatal cattle disease, also called 'mad cow disease'.

Drought A long period of time when there is little or no rainfall that leads to a severe shortage of water.

Developed world The wealthier countries of the world, in which there are highly developed industries.

Developing world The poorer countries of the world, which rely more on farming than industry.

Erosion The wearing away of rock and soil by things such as wind and rain.

Evaporation The process by which water turns to water vapour. This happens when water is heated.

Family planning The control of the number of children in a family.

Famine A situation in which there is a severe shortage of food.

Famine relief Emergency food and medical supplies donated to people in need. It is only a short-term solution.

Fertilisers Substances added to soil to make plants grow faster or bigger. They can be natural, but many farmers use artificial chemical fertilisers that can cause water pollution.

Foot-and-mouth disease A disease that affects animals such as cattle and pigs.

Genetically modified (GM) crops Crops that have been altered artificially to give them new properties, for example resistance to pesticides.

Global warming The gradual rise in the Earth's temperature.

High-yield crop A food crop such as rice or wheat that has been developed to produce more food than naturally occurring plants of the same type.

Intercropping A way of farming in which two or more different crops are grown side by side.

Irrigation The supply of water to farmland through pipes or channels.

Locust An insect that lives in warm regions of the world and travels in swarms.

Nutrients The chemicals that plants and animals need to live and grow.

Pesticides Farm chemicals used to deal with pests such as insects, fungi and weeds that kill or compete with crops.

Slum An area of shacks built by poor people, also called a shanty town.

Sustainable Something that can be done over and over again with no significant effect on the environment.

Vaccination The process of protecting a person or animal from certain diseases. The vaccine is usually a liquid given by injection.

World Bank An international organisation which provides loans for development projects around the world.

Find out more

www.fairtrade.org.uk
Click on this site to learn all about fair trade and the fair trade logo. You will find out what fair trade products you can buy and there are even fair trade recipes to try.

www.foei.org
The site of Friends of the Earth International: learn all about their campaigns on topics, such as GM crops and forest conservation.

www.fao.org/wfd
Read about World Food Day and how you can play a part in helping to solve the problem of world hunger.

www.msc.org
The Marine Stewardship Council's site has lots of information on fishing and how it can be made less environmentally destructive. Discover which fish are best to buy and eat.

www.oxfam.org
Find out what Oxfam is doing to help people escape from poverty, suffering and hunger. Find out how you can help.

www.itdg.org
Information from 'Practical Solutions' (formerly ITDG) about the causes of hunger and details of many projects that are helping people escape from poverty.

Index